AMERICA NEEDS

A

DREAM

2nd Edition

A Closer look at the DREAM Act and
what it means for America.

MIKE J. QUINN

For information contact:

Mike@thedishwashersson.org

http://www.thedishwashersson.org

ISBN: 9781075617379

Dedication

To my DREAMer daughter Adriana, and all the other DREAMers in our country who are already Americans at heart.

Contents

The History
of the DREAM Act

The original version of the DREAM Act was introduced on April 25, 2001, by Representative Luis Gutiérrez, a Democrat. It was called the "Immigrant Children's Educational Advancement and Dropout Prevention Act of 2001. This bill had 34 co-sponsors and would have allowed illegal immigrant students to apply to be protected from deportation and then apply for lawful permanent residency if they met specific criteria.

One month later, on May 21, 2001, Gutiérrez's version of the bill was scrapped in favor of a more limited version entitled "Student Adjustment Act of 2001," introduced by Republican Representative

Chris Cannon. This version of the bill lowered age eligibility to 21 years of age and saw 62 co-sponsors.

On August 1, 2001, a mirror bill to the "Student Adjustment Act of 2001" was introduced in the Senate by Senator Orrin Hatch, also a Republican. This legislation was the first bill given the short title of "Development, Relief, and Education for Alien Minors Act" or "DREAM Act."

The text of the bill made its way into various other immigration-related bills, including the Comprehensive Immigration Reform Act of 2006 and the Comprehensive Immigration Reform Act of 2007. With the failure of these comprehensive reform bills, Senator Richard Durbin, Democrat from Illinois, made it his mission to pass the bill in 2007.

In September 2007, Durbin filed to place the DREAM Act as an amendment to the 2008 Department of Defense Authorization Bill. Facing mounting criticism, Durbin tabled the amendment in favor of a re-written DREAM Act amendment to the Defense Bill. In consideration of his opponents, all language regarding in-state tuition was removed from the amendment, and an age cap of 30 was put in place for potential beneficiaries.

Military leaders endorsed the bill, which included the promise of resident status to members of the military, as a means of boosting recruitment at a time when voluntary military enlistment was at an all-time low.

On October 18, 2007, Durbin, along with Republican co-sponsors Charles Hagel of Nebraska and Richard Lugar of Indiana, introduced the DREAM Act as S. 2205. Although nearly identical to the revised amendment to the Defense Bill. Opponents continued to cite previous arguments, and so a vote was scheduled October 24 to bring the DREAM Act up for debate, but that vote failed to get the 60 votes it needed to become law.

Senate opponents cited a variety of reasons for their opposition. Some labeled the DREAM Act as amnesty and would encourage chain migration and further illegal immigration. Others stated that the

DREAM Act, though a worthy idea, should be enacted only as part of comprehensive immigration reform, which we have all witnessed over many years, would mean certain death for the bill.

Senator Kay Bailey Hutchison, who previously opposed the DREAM Act, announced that she had expressed reservations to Durbin and he had made a verbal commitment to work with her to make changes that she saw necessary to obtain greater Republican support. In response, Durbin announced he would be glad to re-write the bill per Hutchison's suggestions should debate for the DREAM Act begin.

Her changes would mandate that illegal immigrant students should be allowed to hold a temporary student visa with a renewable work permit instead of conditional permanent residency. Although 52 Senators voted in favor of considering the DREAM Act, this was eight votes short of breaking filibuster, and the legislation was not considered."

In 2008, after failing several times to get the backing of Congress, Republican Kay Bailey Hutchison, announced she would work with the authors of the DREAM Act to make it more acceptable for Republicans.

This DREAM Act (v2.0) was then reintroduced to Congress, having been trimmed again by Republican lawmakers, putting their conservative positions on it. Under this version of the DREAM Act, immigrants could qualify in part, by meeting the following requirements:

- Be between the ages of 12 and 35 at the time the law is enacted

- Arrived in the United States before the age of 16

- Resided continuously in the United States for at least 5 consecutive years since the date of their arrival

- Graduated from a U.S. high school or obtained a General Education Diploma

- Good moral character

In addition to the temporary residency, illegal immigrant students who qualified would also be able to apply for student loans and work-study, but would not be eligible for Pell grants. In certain circumstances, the person could lose temporary immigration residency if he or she did not meet the educational or military service requirement within six-years, or if they committed any crimes (other than those considered non-drug related misdemeanors). If an individual were convicted of a major crime or drug-related infraction, they would automatically lose the six-year temporary residence status and be immediately subject to deportation.

The DREAM Act v2.0 still failed to pass a vote in 2009.

Back to the drawing board it went, and Republicans came up with a new version of the DREAM Act, which included numerous changes. The DREAM Act, along with a repeal of "Don't Ask, Don't Tell," was incorporated into the National Defense Authorization Act for the Fiscal Year 2011.

On September 21, 2010, the Senate filibuster of the bill was maintained having failed to get the 60 votes to stop the filibuster and continue the progress of the bill.

The following day, Durbin, along with Richard Lugar, introduced the bill once again, but since they were the only two senators who co-sponsored the bill, it was defeated again.

Less than a month later, on November 16, President Barack Obama and top Democrats pledged to introduce the Dream Act into the House by November 29. The House of Representatives passed the DREAM Act on December 8, 2010, but because of Republican opposition, the bill failed to reach the 60-vote threshold necessary to end debate on the Senate floor.

Much needs to be said for the resilience and courage in the face of incredible opposition that the backers of the DREAM Act refused to let it die, but the Republicans continue their fierce opposition to such a noble and truly American idea.

On May 11, 2011, then Senate Majority Leader Harry Reid reintroduced the DREAM Act in the Senate. Some Republicans who had supported the bill in the past, including Sen. John Cornyn of Texas, Jon Kyl of Arizona, John McCain of Arizona, and Lindsey Graham of South Carolina, withheld their votes, objecting that such a bill should not be passed without increasing immigration enforcement. Reid indicated that he would consider adding a workplace enforcement measure in the DREAM Act that would require every employer to use E-Verify. President Obama supported the bill as one of his efforts to reform the U.S. immigration system.

In July 2011, the state of California enacted the California DREAM Act, giving undocumented immigrant students access to private college scholarships for state schools. In August, the state of Illinois authorized a privately funded scholarship plan for children of immigrants both documented and undocumented. The individual States were once again, making it their job to legislate immigration in the face of federal abdication of their responsibility.

This latest version of the DREAM Act (v 4.0) is still too generous for the Republicans to sign pass in Congress. It appears they are proving to be an increasingly negative obstacle to getting any bill through Congress that will legalize even the cream of the crop of our currently undocumented citizens.

If only the GOP could remember that in 1798 the Republican Party was included with Catholics as the first class of people to be purposely excluded in our first immigration laws. Maybe if they remembered that they, too, were discriminated against and unfairly restrained from attaining their American heritage, then they might have a change of heart.

On June 15, 2012, President Barack Obama announced that his administration would stop deporting undocumented immigrants who match specific criteria included in the proposed DREAM Act. DACA gives the government prosecutorial discretion, providing temporary relief from deportation (deferred action) and work authorization to certain young undocumented immigrants brought to the United States as children.

On August 15, 2012, the U.S. Citizenship and Immigration Services (USCIS) began accepting applications under the Obama administration's new Deferred Action for Childhood Arrivals (DACA) program. Thousands applied for the new program. Because DACA was designed in large measure to address the immigration status of the same people as the DREAM Act, the two programs are often debated together, with some making little distinction between them and others focusing on the difference between the DREAM Act's legislative approach in contrast to the implementation of DACA through executive action.

Encouraged by DACA, a new approach was needed to resurrect the DREAM Act. It was adopted by the "Gang of Eight" a bi-partisan group of senators who hoped that with unified support, the legislation would be supported by the Republicans, who withheld much-needed support for the past versions of the bill. With a new title, "Border Security, Economic Opportunity, and Immigration Modernization Act of 2013, they tried again.

The members of the Gang of Eight consists of the following four Democratic and four Republican senators:

Sen. Michael Bennet, D-CO

Sen. Dick Durbin, D-IL

Sen. Jeff Flake, R-AZ

Sen. Lindsey Graham, R-SC

Sen. John McCain, R-AZ

Sen. Robert Menendez, D-NJ

Sen. Marco Rubio, R-FL

Sen. Chuck Schumer, D-NY

The Senate Judiciary Committee held hearings on the bill in April 2013 and was placed on the Senate calendar. On June 27, 2013, the Senate passed the bill with a 68-32 margin. (all 52 Democrats, both Independents and 14 Republicans voted in favor of the bill.) The bill was unfortunately not presented to the floor for a vote by the Republican-controlled House of Representatives and died in the 113th Congress.

The American Dream and Promise Act of 2019 is the first bill introduced in the 116th Congress that would offer a path to legal status for DREAMers. This bill is an expansive proposal, going beyond DREAM Act bills that have been pending in Congress in one form or another since 2001. While this bill has no chance of becoming law, it is intended to serve two purposes:

1) Reset the basis for future immigration negotiations.

2) Show a commitment from House Democrats that they will prioritize action on behalf of DREAMers and other unauthorized immigrants with U.S. ties.

Although this bill passed the Democratic-controlled House of Representatives, it is currently languishing in the same waste bin as all the other previous versions of the DREAM Act as the

Republicans refuse to even take up the bill on the Senate floor for fear they'd have to vote on it and reveal their true anti-immigrant colors.

As of January 2017, 740,000 people have registered through DACA.

On September 5, 2017, the Trump administration rescinded the DACA program, but the courts are temporarily putting the brakes on any future attacks on immigrants for the moment.

The DREAM
Act Today

There are rumors of a new DREAM Act developed by a Republican, but why would this version of the DREAM Act pass through Congress when others didn't? Perhaps having a resentful Democratic veto is precisely what the Republicans are hoping for because then they will be able to blame the Democrats for this stalemate, conveniently forgetting all of their previous acts of sabotage.

The Republicans know they have done a great job of demonizing the Latino population. They cannot provide a path for undocumented immigrants to receive citizenship, even ten years from now, for fear the Latino voters will long remember the hardship they had to endure because of their shameful conservative attitudes and harsh anti-immigrant positions. New Latino voters will become a large and powerful anti-Republican force.

The DREAM Act, as it stands right now, has been crafted by both Democrats and Republicans. If that won't help it pass through Congress, it stands to reason nothing will. Evidence of this position is clear from recent comments of some Republicans who are still labeling the latest, most stripped down version of the DREAM Act as "back door amnesty."

A recent example of the persecution of immigrants happened on September 5, 2017, As acting Secretary of Homeland Security Elaine Duke rescinded the 2012 DACA memorandum and announced a "wind down" of DACA. Effective immediately, no new applications for DACA would be accepted. DACA beneficiaries whose status was due to expire before March 5, 2018, were permitted to renew their status for an additional two years if they applied by October 5, 2017. Any person for whom DACA would have expired as of March 6, 2018, would no longer have deferred action or employment authorization.

In early June 2019, with strong support from organized labor, the Dreamers, Latinos, and Asian-American groups, the U.S. House of Representatives approved legislation to keep an estimated two million Dreamers and hundreds of thousands of Temporary Protected Status beneficiaries in the U.S.

The 237-187 vote, with seven Republicans joining all 230 voting Democrats, sent the measure (HR6) to the Senate, where right-wing lawmakers, including Mitch "the Grim Reaper" McConnel, are attempting to block it. McConnel has vowed that no vote on this bill will take place in the Senate where the Republicans hold a majority. The bill is now in political limbo.

With the current muzzling of DACA and the latest DREAM Act put on hold by Mitch McConnel, I urge you to read the article below on the DREAM Act and what it says about the bill, in its latest iteration. How could any sane person see this as a gift that will be used by masses of undeserving people? It still doesn't guarantee anyone citizenship- - just the opportunity to apply for it. These will be smart, ambitious, strong, sacrificing people of high moral character who show a high probability for positive social and economic growth. Who wouldn't want these fine young people to be a part of their nation?

Why we need
the DREAM Act

Today, hi-tech entrepreneurs, college grads, and military personnel who are not citizens of this country have no real incentive to help make this country better. When these immigrants get their final notice to leave, they will inevitably return to where they came and work to make those countries stronger, more competitive and leave a hole in our efforts to retain world economic leadership.

There are many negative consequences of imposing immigration duties on our police force who are untrained in immigration law:

- Children separated from their families.

- Americans harassed unnecessarily.

- Crops are being left to rot in the fields.

- Schools are reporting drops in attendance.

- Crimes are going unreported.

- Small businesses will close.

Local economies will have fewer customers to purchase goods.

There are also embarrassing international consequences for foreign investors like the huge Mercedes-Benz fiasco. Alabama spent considerable time and resources lobbying Mercedes-Benz to put a manufacturing plant in their state, but thanks to their reinvented immigration laws, they arrested one of the company's executives while he was driving to work one day. Persecution of foreign investors is no model for promoting investment in our country, nor is it an example of how to lead our weak economy to a speedy recovery.

We all benefit from the contributions these fine people make to our society. American Veterans who sacrificed their best years to protect our nation deserve to live in our country. For these people, citizenship is not a gift-- It is a reward.

Students (grads), spend more money in their communities and give back more than they receive. They are also more likely to start businesses, create jobs, and support our economy for the next 40 years before they retire. Why would we want to send them back to another country?

Military Personnel

If someone is willing to sacrifice the best years of their lives in the service of our nation and even put their life on the line to defend us, then not offering them citizenship and not allowing them to be a part of the democratic process for which they made that sacrifice is a crime of the highest magnitude.

A servicemember's sacrifice is a demonstration of their commitment to our society and our nation. A good faith return of appreciation for this should represent the respect of a grateful nation. Everyone who has served in the armed services of the United States of America should receive all of the benefits and responsibilities of this country. Ask any veteran.

Respect and gratitude are not all there is to this subject. If we are not willing to follow through with our commitment to immigrant servicemembers, what would prevent them from reneging on their dedication to us? A half-committed soldier is not the person anyone would want as a team member on patrol. Our men and women need to trust 100% that the person next to them is going to be there when the stuff hits the fan.

Having non-citizens in our military at all could pose a direct conflict of interest with our national security. Which country will that person side with if we should go to war in their home country? We have only to look toward Iraq and Afghanistan to see recent examples of how our military lacked trust and commitment while working with soldiers of "friendly" countries.

Will they be effective in their mission in their home countries knowing that soon they will be sent back home as civilians and have to face their neighbors for the actions they performed while their allegiances bound them to us?

We owe it to ourselves and to the immigrant servicemember that all military personnel should be citizens on the day they graduate basic training.

Students

The United States' college and university system attracts some of the best students from all over the world. A US degree is often built on cutting edge information, developed in this country, and is a highly sought after commodity.

Often students will intern at companies within their fields of study, gaining practical experience in their area of expertise. This marriage of education and experience makes them exceptional candidates for the workforce and creates some of the most sought after graduates in the world.

We also have a vibrant community of investors who are always looking for the next big thing. Large complexes of industries are often set up near colleges and universities that are known for excellence in a specific field.

Combine the elements of education, corporations, and investment into one localized and easy to access area, and we have created a very nurturing environment for product and company creation and is precisely what sets us so far ahead of other industrialized nations. This lead won't last long as other countries are catching on to this idea and are implementing the same strategy themselves.

If we make it a priority to send these educated and talented people back home, other countries will capitalize on our investments, and we will literally be training our competitors.

As far as US investors go, they will be reluctant to pump money into a future product or company, knowing all of their investment in time and money will be going back home with the founders when they get asked to leave.

This uncertain future outlook will stifle US investment and product creation, slow job creation, and as a result, our economy will suffer. Add to this misery, the creation of a highly competent competitor in another nation, and the recipe for US economic success is doomed. This is where our "America First" strategy bites us on our own butt.

Since we are the ones who trained the student and gave them access to our considerable knowledge base and investment resources, shouldn't we also be the ones who benefit from this ecosystem?

If taking in immigrants is our national heritage, college graduates could be considered the cream of the crop. How could we not want them?

Are we so afraid of internal competition that we will purposely reduce our talent pool while at the same time raising the skills of our competitor's? If so, we might as well raise a flag of surrender right now. Our American can-do attitude got us where we are today, and if we are to stay ahead of the global competition, we will need to step up our competitive game, not step it down.

Benefits
for America

The United States' college and university system attracts some of the best students from all over the world. A US degree is often built on cutting edge information, developed in this country, and is a highly sought after commodity.

Often We have known for years that as our baby boomers age out of the workforce, we will not have the numbers of people to replace them. The number of births in the U.S. dropped by 2 percent between 2017 and 2018, to 59 births per 1,000 women ages 15 to 44. This lack of repopulation in our native population will create multiple crises in many industries and negatively impact our economy as a whole.

The Social Security system will become inundated with increasing numbers of people taking out of the system much more than they will be putting in.

Retiring health care workers will leave massive shortages of trained doctors and staff as our population bubble retires, lives longer, and needs more medical attention than at any other time in history.

Many other industries will experience this same crisis as well. Our economic engine will soon run out of gas.

Next comes inflation. What we think will be enough for retirement today will be woefully inadequate for our needs in the next ten to twenty years without a plentiful supply of highly trained people to take our places. Fewer doctors will charge more per visit due to undersupply and over demand alone.

If we allowed immigrant College graduates to

stay in the U.S., with their whole lives ahead of them, they would be caring for us and paying into a system decades before they will receive any benefits. With our aging baby boomer's life expectancy being higher than in any other time in history, soon imported labor will be our lifeblood. We have always needed immigrants to give us a more opulent lifestyle than we otherwise could afford. We need them now, and we will be glad they are here tomorrow as long as we don't chase them away today.

The non-partisan Congressional Budget Office estimated this reform bill would have reduced the U.S. fiscal deficit by US$197 billion over the next ten years and by $700 billion by 2033. The report also states that, if the bill had become law, U.S. wages would have been 0.1 percent lower in 2023 and 0.5 percent higher in 2033 than under current law. The Social Security Administration also said that it would help add $276 billion in revenue over the next ten years while costing only $33 billion.

To put this in perspective, in 2019 the US will spend over 25 Billion dollars on CBP & ICE for our government's radical immigration enforcement policies.

The DREAM Act suppression is just a Republican ploy to deny new political competition into society. It harms our country and sets us up for further problems in the years to come and costs our economy more money than the Republicans say undocumented immigrants cost us.

Conclusion

L et us not forget that the DREAM Act is now, and has always been--a compromise. Citizenship for all the people who are effectively US citizens right now is what we need. These undocumented immigrants are already here, working, creating jobs, and supporting our economy with inexpensive products and services that help our shrinking dollar go further. They are also fighting by our side and paying the ultimate sacrifice to help us defend freedom in countries around the globe.

With any DREAM Act, we sacrifice most of the hardworking, day-in, day-out, working-class immigrants to push through legislation that will help the few who are fighting for our country or are the best educated. Let us not forget that with this benefit also comes the responsibility and obligation to make our country better.

I urge you to let Congress know how you feel.

Also, let's not forget about the Congressmen and women who are supposed to be making these laws.

Any logical person would conclude that if both Democrats and Republicans can't pass laws our country needs, after eighteen years of trying, we cannot look to them for the leadership they promised us when we elected them.

What happens when our bosses think we are no longer competent to do our jobs?

We get fired. . . .

Trump, Congress, you are on notice

Stop persecuting immigrants and pass an immigration bill that is good for the country, as well as the immigrant, or you will not be invited back for another term. Our nation's history has shown that vilifying an immigrant community is a short-term win for votes, but ultimately a long-term loss for legislation in a country that prides itself on being the "land of the free" and host to the "American Dream."

We are ALL immigrants and denying rights to newcomer immigrants insults the struggles our forefathers went through to get the rights and privileges we currently posess.

If Congress doesn't pass the DREAM Act the

people who will be filling their current positions will know that the same fate will apply to them, but instead of having eighteen years to get something done, they should have just one term.

- We need our economy to run more efficiently.

- We need healthcare that is affordable for all.

- We need all of our citizens to be legal and represented in our government.

- We need to stop persecuting people because of the color of their skin.

- And above all,

- We need people in a government who can play nicely with each other and help solve our nation's problems.

- Braggarts, posers, and frauds need not apply…

About
the Author

Mike J. Quinn is an American citizen with a multinational family. He has also managed restaurants for over 25 years and worked with immigrants from many different nations, and with many different immigration statuses. He has been working to unify his family in the United States for over ten years.

He is also the Author of "The Dishwasher's Son" a novel about an American teenager and Arizona Minuteman volunteer who accidentally gets deported along with some of his coworkers when the restaurant he works in gets raided by ICE. While in Mexico, he runs into an uncle, and together they learn the truth about his father's disappearance. Because of his deportation, he must sneak back into his own country using many of the same methods he has been learning to defend against as a Minuteman volunteer. Along the way he must also learn to deal with the Mexican heritage he has denied his whole life.

DREAM Act debate index

When encountering these arguments, there will be two distinct people on the other side of the debate.

1) An ultra-conservative who hates immigrants and wants to return to an all-white dominated America.

2) Someone who has listened to the arguments the ultra-conservatives and and has chosen that position because it sounded logical.

When talking to the second group, be kind and courteous. They may change their positions when confronted with more logical and humanitarian arguments. When talking with the first group, you will know by their stubborn insistence that, even in the face of superior logic and realistic statistics, they still hold fast to their dogma, it is my belief you will not change their minds and should just give up. There is a saying: The only person dumber than someone who thinks they know it all, is the person who is arguing with them.

Good luck, and persevere. These kids are depending on us.

Arguments against the DREAM

It is a gift to undocumented aliens

Everyone in the DREAM Act eligibility list will have come to the US as a minor. They were brought here without any choice. And the benefits of this bill are not available to every child that came across the border with their family. They have to be smart, studious, hard working, goal oriented, or be willing to put their life on the line for the privilege of being allowed to apply for a green card. Citizenship will have to be applied for later and they will have to qualify for that all over again. This is not a gift — it's a reward for being smart, committed and selfless. These are the best of the best. Isn't that what the conservatives want?

It encourages more illegal immigration

How can this bill encourage more illegal immigration when you will be screened heavily for eligibility and go through multiple rounds of paperwork and background checks to qualify? Wouldn't that be a huge waste of time to come here, learn English, and study for years and still not become eligible? Sounds more like a disincentive. Becoming eligible will take hard work and sacrifice. No one will be guaranteed. To qualify for the DREAM Act, immigrants will have earned it.

It will cost billions in tax dollars to US taxpayers.

It is already costing Americans Billions of dollars every year to house and feed the thousands of immigrants being unfairly incarcerated at immigration detention centers around the country. Getting them out of these for profit detention centers and into the economy is what will make the DREAM Act pay for itself.

It takes away education spots for American students.

The college and university system has been operating on a competitive basis where you must apply for the ability to attend any particular school and you are selected based upon your academic qualifications. No university selects students by virtue of their national origin. It is a well known fact that Universities are heavily incentivized to pick the students with the best chances of becoming donating alumni. DREAM Act students will have to apply and compete for spots just like everyone else.

The immigrants could eventually petition for their relatives to get residency causing chain migration.

Aren't we ALL here because of chain migration? Besides, relative visas are not even involved in this process and are a completely separate issue.

Service could be the only way to gain residency for the underprivileged.

So what is the point here? Veterans aren't good enough to be citizens? Military service is service to our country and all service members should be respected and given every benefit our society has to offer. Just ask any Veteran.

The DREAM Act is amnesty.

> Amnesty: *an act of forgiveness for past offenses, especially to a class of persons as a whole.*

To forgive someone for something that is not his or her fault, is not a sin. The President of the United States pardons people every year for worse offenses. Some of them committed murder and crimes much more severe than being brought here against their will as children. If amnesty were a sin, would we allow our President to provide it to whomever he chooses? There are other words in the dictionary much more offensive than amnesty that are committed by our government every day: arrogance, ignorance, bigotry, uncompromising, prejudice, insulting, degrading, dishonoring, bullying . . .

Immigrants will take jobs away from Americans.

Very few people have their jobs taken away from them that weren't going to lose them anyway. Do you mean they will compete in the job market? Yep, they will. Have you ever applied for a job? What did you do? You filled out an application, built a resume, distributed it to many employers and tried to sing the best song you could in order to wow your future boss. You are competing on talent, education, experience and pay scale. Any one of these could knock you out of the game. It's hard. There's a lot of competition out there. If that's what it takes, then that's what it takes and there's nothing anyone can do about it short of ruining democracy and free enterprise and kill what little competitive edge we have in the world. Force an employer to take a citizen over an immigrant, force him to pay more, and watch his cost of goods and services drown out his profit. Raising his prices cuts him out of the market. Meanwhile, a less than worthy employee who knows he has his job sewn up because his employer has to take him, his productivity dives through the floor. He has no incentive to produce. He gets paid no matter what. What kind of a society is that called again?

They still broke the law. What about illegal don't you understand?

First, Entering Without Inspection, or overstaying your visa, the two ways to get into this country illegally, are minor civil offenses. They are like traffic tickets.

Secondly, they were minor children who followed their families into this country, or didn't know how to take care of maintaining their paperwork themselves. If a parent pushing a stroller gets busted for shoplifting a package of diapers, do we prosecute the baby too? They were with their parent, but the baby doesn't get into trouble. Why? Because it wasn't their fault and we are not stupid.

Logical Arguments
for the DREAM

These are some of the many reasons America would benefit by passing this bill:

1. Educated immigrants will add much needed tax revenues for our country.

2. Almost half of all Fortune 500 companies were founded by immigrants or children of immigrants.

3. Educated Immigrants have a lower instance of violent crime.

4. Educated immigrants add to the consumer base, buying houses, cars and helping to support our economy.

5. Educated immigrants will be young and able to contribute to the social security system for

decades after the baby boomers have cleaned it out.

6. Educated immigrants often have ties to their mother countries making them great candidates to assist US companies in global markets.

7. Veterans have learned to work well with others, respect leadership.

8. Veterans often learn valuable trades and gain excellent experience and will be great employees, neighbors and friends.

Veterans are often experts in using weapons so you should be very polite to them. (Just checking to see if you were still reading this) I'm not kidding about the "being polite" part. Veterans earned our respect and we owe them a debt of gratitude for putting their lives on the line so we can have the freedoms we enjoy every day. Refusing them citizenship is the ultimate betrayal from a "grateful nation."

If you liked this book, please give it a review on Amazon.com. The more people that are familiar with the information gathered here will help put pressure on our Conservative opponents. And don't forget to vote at every election and protest for our immigrant's rights whenever possible. Your presence and your vote will make a difference.